TABLE OF CONTENTS

GW01311919

WHAT IS MYSTERY SHOPPING?

What is it, you ask? I tell my friends who are curious about it that mystery shopping is when companies pay you to act like a "normal" person and evaluate their business. The idea is that companies want to know what's really happening in their retail stores, restaurants, and other establishments, so they pay mystery shoppers to go in and evaluate their experiences, while acting like a regular customer. The "mystery" is that the companies being evaluated don't know about it. Well, their managers and owners know and are paying to have an evaluation done, but they don't know which customer is the one doing the actual assignment. The employees do not know if or when a mystery shopper is coming. That's where YOU step in!

How It Works

The manager or owner of an establishment hires a third-party mystery shopping company to perform the unbiased evaluation. The mystery shopping company then hires you. Your identity remains anonymous so that you can remain unbiased. The company usually creates a pretend scenario for you and asks you to check on specific words an employee might say, how specific merchandise and signs are displayed in a store, or how a certain food item tastes. The client and mystery shop company create a list of areas they want the shopper to check on. After visiting the business, the shopper then writes a report, uploads any receipts online, and submits everything to the company. All expenses are then reimbursed, and everyone lives happily ever after! Well, usually.

After you write your report, employees who have provided exceptional service are often rewarded with a special bonus. Any employees whom you have identified as less than ideal usually receive additional training to get them up to standards. In other words, the company values your opinions and takes action on your feedback.

Sometimes you'll be asked to make a purchase, which you will be reimbursed for, but you're also asked to check on customer service, cleanliness, employee knowledge, merchandise selection and displays, the manager's interaction with employees, and quality. If the assignment is for a restaurant, for example, your meal will be paid for (reimbursed). You will also be paid to write the report, which is often a short questionnaire online with brief narrative.

Variety

It's a lot of fun! Mystery shopping is one of my all-time fave's for getting paid to do something that I'm already doing anyway, like getting an oil change, seeing a movie, or shopping at a store. I've had boring assignments like assessing a post office, and exciting assignments such as getting paid to play at a theme park with my kids! I especially love the restaurant assignments, because it's like getting a free date night with my husband. I could eat out every day for free if I wanted to accept that many assignments. Companies will always pay for your food, and most will pay an additional fee for your written report.

You might be paid to make a phone call to a company to see how their staff handles questions. Hotels often request help from mystery shoppers to make reservations online or over the phone and then cancel them in order to evaluate that entire process. Over the years, I've also accepted assignments from companies that paid me to order items online and then return them. Many times, I've been able to keep the products. You can get a free gym membership, free airline flights, and unlimited products for only a little bit of your time and effort! Each assignment is different and has been carefully designed by the business and the mystery shop company that has hired you.

Speaking of a written report, that's what you'll be creating after you eat that free dinner or buy that free shirt at the store. You will discreetly take notes while you perform your assignment and then, when you return home, you will fill out a form online that the mystery shop company provides for you. It's mostly Yes/No questions with an occasional short paragraph. There is a company, however, which is notorious for requiring their mystery shoppers to write lengthy answers, but they also pay a lot more and have some really cool assignments at hotels, theme parks, and high end restaurants.

Types of Assignments

There are different kinds of mystery shop assignments. Here are few:

Traditional:

The mystery shopper (you) visits a business, pretending to be a "regular" customer. After evaluating certain aspects like customer service, product quality, cleanliness, etc., the shopper writes an unbiased and detailed report that is uploaded to the mystery shop company's website. The company then edits your report to their specifications and shares it with the business that was evaluated. You are then reimbursed for any expenses and paid for your written report.

Telephone Only:

The mystery shopper (you) simply calls a company, pretending to be a regular customer. From the comfort of your home, you take notes on how the employee on the other end of the phone responds to specific questions. You will often be testing friendliness, product knowledge, audio quality, and professionalism. You will write a detailed report and sometimes even record the call on the mystery shop company's internal equipment online. They'll teach you how to do that. You are then paid for your report.

Online Only:

The mystery shopper (you) visits a business website to evaluate ease of purchase, product variety and descriptions, or ease of use with their Live Chat feature to evaluate an employee's ability to answer questions. Sometimes an online purchase is required. When the product arrives, the mystery shopper takes photos of the condition of the product and quality of the packaging. A detailed report and photos are uploaded. You are then reimbursed for the purchase, shipping, and paid for your written report.

Audio & Video:

The mystery shopper (you) visits a business, pretending to be a regular customer. You wear a hidden camera or audio equipment to record your interactions with employees. Sometimes a mystery shop company will provide you with equipment, but more often than not, you will be expected to provide your own. Not every state allows such assignments due to privacy laws, so be sure to double-check with the Reporters Committee for Freedom

of the Press to make sure you are in compliance. You can go to:
www.rcfp.org Both a written report and the recording are submitted by the
mystery shopper online and you are paid.

<u>Reveal:</u>

The mystery shopper (you) visits a business, pretending to be a regular
customer. When an employee says a particular phrase or demonstrates
specific behavior that the client wants to encourage, you reveal yourself as a
mystery shopper and give the employee a prize! The mystery shop company
will ship you prizes before you perform the assignment. The reward could be
cash, a gift card, t-shirt, etc. Sometimes, if no employee has received the
prize, you reveal yourself to the manager to explain what you saw. Either
way, a written report is still uploaded by the shopper after the experience.
This kind of assignment can be a lot of fun! Unfortunately, you are usually
not allowed to perform future assignments at that location because your
identity has now been revealed.

<u>Price Audit:</u>

The mystery shopper (you) visits a business, pretending to be a regular
customer. Discreetly, you either take photos or notes of the prices on various
items. After leaving, you write a detailed report and upload it to the mystery
shop company's website. Some businesses like to use this data to compare
how they are performing against their competition.

Mystery shopping is perfect for anyone who loves to shop and get paid for
things you would probably already spend money on like dining in restaurants,
buying clothes, making purchases online, staying in hotels, or having fun at
amusements parks! It's an honest, legitimate, and fun way to earn money.
You can also feel good, knowing that the information you provide to local
companies and large chains can make a positive difference in how they do
business. You're in control of your schedule, as you can accept or reject
whatever assignments suit your time and lifestyle.

You're really going to enjoy it. This book is designed to help you get started.

Online Course

During the 30 years I have been a mystery shopper, so many people have
asked me about what I do and how they can do it too. If you enjoy taking
online courses, you might be interested in taking my class on "How To Get

Paid To Eat, Shop, & Play" at www.LifelongLearningEducation.com

You can go online to learn more about the fun course that walks you through the process and gets you set up to start earning money and getting free things! For every course you take, you earn a free gift certificate that you can use towards another course! We currently offer classes on "How To Write & Publish Your Book", "Morning Ritual Magic", "Nutrition For Better Health", "Spanish For Medical Professionals", "Meditation & Mindfulness", "Life Hacks", and "Daily Drops of Inspiration." More courses are currently in development!

IS IT LEGIT?

In a word, YES! Mystery shopping is not an urban legend! It has been around for decades in the United States and has also been called Secret Shopping or Shopping Incognito. It began in the 1940's as a way for companies to evaluate how their employees were doing. A mystery shopper was even featured in a movie in 1941 called *The Devil and Miss Jones*! Even before that, it has been rumored that kings would dress up like commoners to wander around the kingdom and hear what was being said about them, as well as see first-hand what was happening on an everyday basis with the people.

It has now spread to many countries around the world and is a fantastic side-hustle for customers who love free things and want to earn extra income. It has further evolved to include an evaluation of customer satisfaction. Competition can be very fierce out there, so companies currently want to know if they are doing everything possible to get new customers, as well as retain them for future visits.

Mystery shoppers are everyday people who want to either earn some extra money on the side or get free stuff or both! Most mystery shoppers accept assignments as a part-time gig, although I have met people over the years that do it as their full-time income. If you love to shop, this could be your dream. job. You're not paid as an employee, but instead, you accept assignments from companies as an Independent Contractor.

Mystery shopping provides something known as the "sentinel effect." When a business hires a mystery shop company to perform an assignment, they often tell their employees to be on their best behavior. They never know when you're going to arrive, so the "threat" of an evaluator's arrival keeps everyone on their toes. Sometimes a manager doesn't tell the employees about a potential mystery shop assignment so that he/she can document suspected bad behavior through an unbiased third party.

Certifications

Being certified by The Mystery Shopping Providers Association will get you more jobs, but it's not required. You take simple tests and earn a silver or gold certification from their nationally recognized organization. A simple place to start is at www.mysteryshop.org. There are other organizations out there as well, like www.volition.com which provide helpful information and list trustworthy companies. They offer conferences and additional training, but they're not necessary in order to get assignments.

Scams

Mystery shopping is a reputable and well-established method that many companies use to measure customer service, consistency, and product quality. That's the good news. The bad news is that there ARE scam-artist companies out there, so keep reading and I'll help you steer clear of them.

Some companies are definitely more reputable than others, so you want to be careful which ones you choose to work with. There's no need to pay for a list of mystery shopping companies, although you'll find many websites that will try to get you to do just that. Never pay for a list. Never pay to sign up for assignments. If you're being asked to pay money to them, you're being scammed and it's not a legitimate mystery shopping company.

A reputable bank will never approach you randomly and offer to pay you obscene amounts of money to test their services by giving you a check and having you run it through your account. That's a famous scam. and a definite red flag. Never trust a Nigerian "prince" or any of those other famous email scams that have been around for decades.

A legitimate mystery shop company will never ask for your credit card number. That's also a red flag that the company is setting you up for a scam. Be wary of companies that advertise on Craig's List or college campuses in attempt to recruit shoppers. Everything you need is right here in this book!

REGISTERING WITH COMPANIES

Which Companies?

Before you can get an assignment, you have to register with a mystery shopping company. Some companies specialize in only one or two kinds of assignments, so I highly recommend applying for several at the same time. For example, I'm registered with a mystery shopping company that only does oil changes, so after I've driven about 3000 miles on my car, I simply call them up and tell them I'm ready for another assignment. Another company I work with only does movie theater assignments, while others specialize in amusement parks. I just let them know when I'm ready for some fun. Many companies, however, offer a variety of assignments, so you'll be able to register and instantly get a lot of variety from them.

ONLY work with reputable companies. When you're new in this industry, I know it's hard to know which mystery shop companies are the good ones! Included in this book is a large list of companies that are known to be good; however, even good ones can go downhill with poor management, so do a quick Google search on the company before you register with them. You can do a Google search with the name of the company and then the word "scam." to see if anything comes up. A red flag is if a company is brand new. Stick with the strong companies that have been around for years. There are plenty of trustworthy companies to work with.

For your convenience, I've provided a gigantic list of mystery shop companies in this book! I have worked with many of them over the years. I definitely have my favorite ones. While I try to keep the list updated and relevant, changes can happen quickly in the industry, so please forgive any errors and let me know about them! Thanks!

How To Register

Once you have found a mystery shopping company that is credible and legitimate, you will go on to their website. Their home page is often a portal for both clients and shoppers. For example, you might see a menu item that says something like, "Become a client" and another one that says, "Become a shopper." Click on the one that looks like the shopper entrance. The other one for clients or customers is for businesses who want to pay the mystery shopping company to do an evaluation of their business.

You should see a place to click on in order to register as a mystery shopper for that company. Just follow the prompts and begin answering the questions. If you have all of your documents ready in advance, it should only take you 15-20 minutes to fill out their forms. If you need to prepare your documents, it could take you as much as an hour to complete everything.

Documents include things you will need to upload, such as a resume, your driver's license, a passport, and a sample report. Every mystery shopping company handles onboarding a little differently, but those are the most common forms of identification that are required. Remember, do not share any of this personal information until you are satisfied that the company is legitimate. The list of companies that are certified by the Mystery Shopping Association is a fantastic place to start. We'll talk about that sample report in just a minute…don't stress out!

Questions Asked

Every company will ask you to provide photo ID, such as a driver's license or passport, so you need to be able to scan those documents into your computer and then upload them during the application process.

They will usually ask if you have previous mystery shopping experience and possibly even ask you to list which companies you have worked for in the past. Don't stress out if you don't have any experience yet. You can give them examples of detailed work you might have done in the past in another industry or simply state how excited you are to begin!

They might ask you about your income, health habits like smoking or drinking, age, marital status, and education level. They're not being nosy; they're trying to determine which assignments might be most suitable for you. Sometimes the mystery shop company's clients are looking for a shopper who is a certain age, gender, or race. Don't be offended. The client is simply trying to get an evaluation performed by the type of customer he wants to attract or is currently serving.

Another piece of personal information you'll be asked for during the registration process is your social security number. Because you will be providing them with work that they pay you for, this is a legitimate request. Often, you will be asked to fill out a W-9 form as an Independent Contractor. Both requests are standard procedure. If you're uncomfortable with the company and something smells fishy, walk away. There are plenty of reputable companies around that you don't need to be spooked by the crummy ones.

During the application process, you might be asked to write a sample report. Don't be scared. They just want to see if you can write correctly and in a detailed manner. I've provided a sample report in this book for you to take a look at. You should NOT copy/paste that into your application. It's just to give you an idea of the kind of detail they're looking for. You'll be writing about a true experience YOU recently had, so be truthful and detailed.

The mystery shopping company is simply looking to see if you can remember details from your experience and then write about them in a compelling manner and without bias. Use your best spelling and grammar, because the company is also looking to see how well you write.

Confirmation

Once you have finished submitting your application, you should receive some kind of email confirmation. The website will usually have you create your own login and password, although some companies create them for you, extending an invitation for you to create a new one if you would like to later. Be sure to record that login and password information somewhere in case you forget!

When you are officially invited into the mystery shopping company's internal website, you will be shown your account information, as well as how to access writing tutorials, manuals that explain company procedures, and how to get assignments. Be sure to read all documents carefully.

A word about verbiage: You work for the mystery shop company, not the client. The "client" is the business that hires the mystery shop company to do the evaluation. The mystery shop company then hires you. You are NEVER allowed to contact the client directly.

TOOLS YOU NEED TO SUCCEED

In order to be successful at any job, you need certain tools. Below is a list and description of some items and characteristics that will allow you to do your best and be your best as a mystery shopper.

Computer

When I first started doing mystery shopping, I would accept assignments and fax in my reports! Yep, I'm THAT old! Nowadays, everything is online, so you'll need some kind of computer or tablet and reliable internet service. If you're doing an overnight assignment at a hotel or on a cruise, you might prefer a laptop. You will be accepting assignments online and submitting your written reports online. Most of the time, the mystery shop companies have already created a form or questionnaire on their website that you simply enter your information on to. It doesn't happen very often, but you might need to use Microsoft Word or Excel, so you'll need to make sure they're installed on your computer. You'll also need an email address.

Bank Account

Some mystery shopping companies will deposit money into your bank account automatically, so you'll need a savings account to use for deposits. More often than not, however, they'll simply mail you a check. Some prefer to use PayPal, but that's not as common either. When you register with the company, they will often give you a choice of which payment method you prefer. You'll just need to make sure everything is set up before you accept your first assignment.

Cell Phone

Some assignments require a cell phone so that you can take digital photos of food, merchandise, displays, store exteriors, etc. You will need to know how to upload images to the mystery shop company's website. The company might also need a photo just to prove that you really were there. In addition, the mystery shopping company needs to be able to get in touch with you by phone in case they have any last-minute information before you complete the assignment or questions they want to ask you after you submit your written report. If an assignment is especially urgent, you might be asked to call in the details for your report. You'll need to make sure you have good cell phone reception and can talk in a quiet, private location. When you write your report, you will be uploading your receipts to the mystery shop company's website, so you'll need to take pictures with a good cell phone camera or else purchase a scanner that connects to your computer.

A word of caution…in case your cell phone battery dies, it's super helpful to have a back-up battery. I've actually had that happen to me! That back-up battery saved me from disaster! It's also good to have a little notebook and pen in case your phone stops working. A wristwatch is also a helpful back-up timekeeper if your cell phone dies and you need to record the timing of things. Timing is especially important when you're doing a restaurant assignment because the client wants to know when food items are ordered and delivered to your table.

Video or Audio Equipment

Some types of assignments might actually require you to record video or audio of your experience at the location. The mystery shop company will let you know what kind of devices are required and, if you don't want to invest in that kind of equipment, then you can simply reject the assignment.

Thirty-six states in the U.S.A. allow hidden video mystery shopping due to one-party consent laws. Fourteen states have two-party consent laws that prohibit video and phone recording (California, Connecticut, Delaware, Florida, Illinois, Maryland, Massachusetts, Michigan, Montana, Nevada, New Hampshire, Pennsylvania, Vermont, Washington.)

If you live in a state that allows these types of assignments and you're interested in doing them, you'll want to invest in a digital voice recorder. Sometimes, the mystery shop company will provide one to you, but more often than not, you'll be expected to get your own. You might even want one just to help you remember everything that happened during your visit to make it easier when it's time to write your report. You definitely don't want anyone to see that you're recording them, so you'll want to get one that allows you to clip a microphone inside your shirt. Don't just put it in your pocket or purse because you won't get good enough sound. Turn it on before you walk into the place of business that you're evaluating! One way to set the time stamp is to simply talk before you walk in, saying something like, "Today is May 4 and it's 2:43 p.m. I'm walking into the Acme Dress Shop on 18 Main Street in Las Vegas, Nevada." It's best to practice before you're actually doing an assignment that requires audio. If all of the technology scares you, you can simply choose not to take the assignment in the first place!

Good Memory

Because you generally won't be able to take notes while you are performing the assignment (unless you run to the restroom), you will also need a good memory! For example, when you enter a restaurant, you'll need to remember the name of the hostess, what she looked like and was wearing, as well as how many other employees were standing by the front door and helping customers. The hostess might engage in friendly chi-chat while she takes you to the table and you'll need to remember the actual words she said when she greeted you and walked with you to your seat.

If all of that stresses you out, this might not be the right job for you. If you can easily remember a few details, you can quickly text those things once she leaves. Sometimes, I'll text information to my husband's phone number so that I can easily retrieve the data when I'm back at home and ready to write the report. I like that better than simply using a note app on my cell phone because each text I write automatically includes a time stamp.

Acting Ability

Acting ability is also a helpful tool. A mystery shop company might ask you to pose as an out-of-town customer visiting a boutique to buy a gift for your mother. They try to create scenarios that sound realistic, so you won't ever be asked to do anything crazy.

Just be calm. If you act nervous, you might arouse suspicion among the employees and you'll be spotted as a mystery shopper.

Clothing

Clothing might also be an important tool to help you "sell" a certain scenario. For example, if you're asked to do a mystery shop assignment in a high-end store or fine dining restaurant, you will need to be able to dress the part and be believable in your demeanor.

Time Management

You also need good time management skills because you will have deadlines to meet. Usually, a mystery shop company will give you a two- or three-day window of time in which to perform your assignment. Sometimes, however, it absolutely has to be done on a specific date and time. Before you accept the assignment, be 100% certain you will be able to do the assignment in the required time. In addition, you need to write your report within 24 hours of finishing the assignment.

Attention To Detail

You definitely need to be detail oriented. You have to be able to notice if an employee's eyes are green or blue, for example, or remember if a waiter served you from your right side or left side when seated at the table. When you get an assignment to a location that has several branches or stores, you need to double-check that you are visiting the correct location. Be sure to read and re-read all of the assignment requirements before you begin the assignment. Also be very familiar with what a mystery shop company expects to be included in your written report. For example, one company may want you to identify the gender and race of an employee, while another company may specifically NOT want you to use those identifiers in your written report!

Self-Control

Finally, the last tool you need is the ability to control your mouth. NEVER should you utter the words "mystery shop" while performing an assignment! If an employee, waiter, or manager overhears you talking to your guest while eating dinner or shopping at a store during your assignment, you will quickly be identified. If you're identified, you might not be paid for your assignment and you will definitely not be allowed to return to that location.

Post-Security Access

This is NOT a required tool, but I thought I'd mention it in case you're interested in doing airport assignments. There are shops and restaurants in airports all over the country that would love for you to evaluate their business! In order to accept an assignment in an airport, you need to have post-security access. You can only get that if you are a pilot, flight attendant, employee, or a ticketed passenger. When I'm getting ready to fly, I go to the websites of mystery shop companies I know schedule those kinds of assignments. Some are A Closer Look and Customer Service Experts. They'll have a list of which airports and store locations have assignments.

Before you accept an airport assignment, be sure that you will have time to write up the report. Most reports are due within 24 hours. I rarely accept an assignment when I a.m. traveling to an exciting destination and beginning my trip, because I know I'll be busy with my travel plans. When I'm flying home, I know I'll have more time when I return, plus I know that my internet is reliable at my house. If you can't guarantee that your travel destination's internet is fast, secure, and reliable, don't accept the assignment. The last thing you want to do when you travel is stress out about an assignment or scramble to find good Wi-Fi.

GETTING ASSIGNMENTS

Anyone Can Do This

Becoming a mystery shopper does not require a college degree or any special license (unless you live in Nevada.) You can already be employed full-time, be a student, or homeworker; they are just looking for regular people from every walk of life. Most companies, however, require a mystery shopper to be at least 18 years of age. In order to accept restaurant assignments, shoppers usually need to be 21 because alcohol is served at the location.

I love the flexibility of mystery shopping because you can choose which assignments to accept, as well as how many you would like to do and when. You'll never get wealthy by doing mystery shop assignments, but you can earn a little while you're having fun and doing things that would normally cost you money! Most shoppers do this as a part-time or as a profitable hobby. If you're interested in doing this as a full-time job, it's definitely possible and still flexible.

Apply To Several Companies

There are large companies that dish out assignments in every state, but there are also smaller companies that only do work in one state. You'll have to do a little research to see which mystery shopping companies operate near you. Most companies specialize in a particular type of store like retail clothing, restaurants, movie theaters, oil changes, or fitness centers. You can choose to work with several different companies at the same time, depending on what kinds of assignments you want to do. You have complete freedom to accept or reject assignments.

Be Proactive

Once you are registered with some companies, there are usually a few different ways to actually get an assignment. Some companies will email or even text you their list of opportunities for the week or month. You then reply to the account manager and tell him/her which assignments you'd like to perform. Many more companies now are posting their assignment opportunities on their website, so you have to be proactive and go see what's available and then officially request the ones you want to do. Sometimes, you can self-assign jobs, but usually there is someone from the company that will provide you with a confirmation and be your point of contact throughout the process.

Nevada Is Unique

If you live in the state of Nevada, you're going to have to jump through a few extra hoops in order to get assignments. I don't know why, other than it's the law. Guess what? I live in Nevada now! You actually have to get a Private Investigator's license in order to do mystery shopping in the state! It's not a big deal though. You simply take a little test, get a background check, and register your fingerprints. That might sound overwhelming, but the people at the Nevada Private Investigators Licensing Board will help walk you through it. Go to https://nevadapilb.glsuite.us

When I first moved to Las Vegas, one of the mystery shop companies here offered to pay for my Private Investigator's license! It never hurts to ask a company for special concessions like that. The worst thing they can say is no. That particular company also offered a writing class for their shoppers to attend in person to help them become better at writing the reports.

Confidentiality

When you sign up to work with a mystery shop company, you will sign a confidentiality statement that prevents you from talking about assignment details with other people. Many times, you will also sign another confidentiality agreement for individual assignments, promising that you will not post commentary or photos on social media after you perform the work.

Demographic Information

Some companies might be looking for a particular kind of shopper, so you'll be asked demographic information about your age, height, weight, income level, education level, etc. For example, a barber shop might only want a male mystery shopper, and a jewelry boutique might want a woman shopper from a high income bracket. Some companies might want a young mother to bring her baby, while many companies will specifically require you to not bring your children along on the assignment. If you're asked to dine in a restaurant, they might require you to order alcohol or ask if you have any food allergies. They will tell you exactly what they need and you need to follow their instructions with complete integrity.

Payment Information

Another part of the application process is setting up your form of payment. Each company will usually have its preferred payment process and will ask you to set that up during registration. For example, some companies prefer to pay via direct deposit into the bank account of your choosing. Others will simply mail you a check, while some prefer PayPal.

You Decide

If you're being offered an assignment that you don't feel comfortable with, don't take it. For example, I don't drink alcohol, so I don't accept bar assignments. Some companies offer restaurant assignments that include a visit to the bar or requiring me to order an alcoholic beverage from the table, so I simply wait for another assignment.

On occasion, you'll see an assignment that asks you to evaluate something odd, such as the color of the napkins. If you think a particular requirement on an assignment is ridiculous, do it anyway. It must be important to the client. If you skip it, you run the risk of not being paid by the mystery shop company. In the case of fine dining restaurants, they often use both black and white napkins and want to know if the waiter is using them properly. If a customer is wearing black pants or a black dress, for example, the waiter is supposed to ask if the customer would like to use a black napkin instead of the regular white one offered to all guests. The black napkin is to avoid getting white lint on the customer's black clothes. It's a 5-star service that shows the restaurant is committed to details. Black napkins also don't show a woman's lipstick. Pretty classy, right?

Blend In

Probably the most important requirement is that you feel comfortable going into a business with an open mind to evaluate what you see and then accurately write a report to explain what you experienced. In your report, you're not writing what you think should have happened; instead, you're simply writing down what did happen. You need to be able to blend in with other customers and quietly observe without standing out.

If you have hot pink hair or you weigh 500 pounds, you're going to stand out and employees might pay close attention to you, so you have to be extremely discreet. Employees can NOT see you taking notes or you will be quickly identified as a mystery shopper and not allowed to return. Because of that, many mystery shoppers will write down their notes in a bathroom stall so that no one can see them writing! Thankfully, employees are used to seeing people text on their cell phones, so you can casually act like you're doing that every now and then and it generally won't set off a red flag for the staff.

Documents

Sometimes, before you are allowed to accept a specific assignment, you will be required to take a little quiz online, ensuring you completely understand the details of the assignment. They'll provide you with a "brief" or document that outlines the specifics. The online quiz usually takes only a few minutes to fill out and is often a simple multiple-choice test. Usually, you're allowed to take the quiz as many times as it takes to get all of the answers correct. Remember, the company WANTS you to succeed with them.

When you accept an assignment, you will usually be given two documents:

1. General guidelines for the assignment. They include payment, store location, deadlines, specific items and behaviors you are looking for, etc.

2. A copy of the questionnaire that you will be using to write your report. That way, you know exactly the things the client is looking for and the questions you'll be required to answer in detail BEFORE you perform the assignment.

Before you perform the assignment, re-read the guidelines so that everything is clear in your mind. You might have previously performed a lunch assignment at a restaurant for a particular mystery shop company, but the dinner assignment might ask for different set of details from the same company. For example, the timing they expect for a casual lunch to be delivered to the table may be different from what they expect during a rush-hour dinner assignment. The reimbursement amount is often much higher at dinner than it is for lunch. Again, read all of the assignment guidelines so you are perfectly clear on the expectations.

Over the years, I have had all kinds of assignments. A few times, a mystery shop company mailed me prizes to award to employees when they exhibited certain behaviors or said specific things to me. That was so much fun to be the bearer of good news and praise! It's called a "Reveal" mystery shop assignment. I've also had assignments where the employees received a cash prize, so I had to pull money out of my bank in the correct bill denomination, but I was quickly reimbursed. That kind of an assignment is pretty rare. If you feel uncomfortable doing something like that, you obviously don't have to accept the assignment! In that specific case, I had worked with the mystery shop company for many years and knew I'd be reimbursed, so I wasn't worried at all. A few times, I was mailed specific posters that I was supposed to present to a manager for him/her to hang up in the store. The most common assignment is simply entering a business, checking things out, and then leaving.

SUPPORT

Documents

When you get an assignment, you'll be given access to documents where you can get answers to your questions. The company wants you to be successful and do a good job, so they're there to help you. Before you do your assignment, you will be given very specific written instructions from the mystery shop company. Be sure to follow them exactly. If you're unsure about something, don't hesitate to call the company.

Scheduler

You will also be given the name of a "scheduler." A scheduler is the person who is directly assigned to help you complete your work. He or she is there to help you through the process and be successful. If you have any questions at all, that is the person to call. They are always available through email, and often through phone calls and texting. Many schedulers work out of their home, so the number they're giving you is often their personal cell phone number. Respect their personal life by not calling them at midnight.

At most companies, a different person is assigned to take care of your payments. If you don't know who that person is and you have questions, your scheduler can let you know whom to contact.

If you like the idea of being a scheduler and coordinating assignments with other shoppers, let the mystery shop company know, as they are almost always looking to hire new people. Schedulers often earn a bonus when they are able to find mystery shoppers for all of the company's assignments during the month. They only earn their bonus once all of the assignments have been completed correctly, so they are highly motivated to help their shoppers do a good job.

Forums

Mystery shopping is a little bit of a lonely job because you're not going into an office and physically gathering around a water cooler to chat with other shoppers. You're a lone wolf out there having fun! If you love the comradery of fellow shoppers, another helpful support can be chatting with other mystery shoppers on Facebook groups or other forums. Just do a quick search to find them. Many mystery shop companies also include a blog or chat area on their internal website. The Mystery Shopping Providers Association also provides chat areas in forums, as well as conferences and opportunities to gather in person.

It's helpful to have a friend or partner to perform assignments together. Most of the dining assignments require you to bring a guest. That second person can help you memorize details or even text them to you as you dine together. The majority of restaurant assignments are for 2 people, although I have been able to eat with 4 on occasion. A few times, I could only accept an assignment if I brought my son, so I simply asked the scheduler if that would be ok. She called the client and got me permission, which was awesome. It's important to note, however, that the payment and reimbursement for the assignment did NOT change with the added person in those situations. The cost of the extra meal came out of my pocket or profit. If you need something, ask. That doesn't mean you'll always get it though!

THE IMPORTANCE OF INTEGRITY

When you accept an assignment, it is EXTREMELY important to keep your commitment. If you forget to do it, cancel at the last minute, or do a terrible job, you're most likely not going to get another assignment. Some companies give you a score based on how well you did. They award assignments to the shoppers with the best rank. You need to be truthful, timely, and a good writer or else they won't give you another assignment.

Contract

Usually, you sign a contract for each assignment, assuring the mystery shop company that you will not disclose your identity to the assigned store before, during, or after the assignment. NEVER use the term "mystery shop" out loud while you are performing the assignment. If an employee overhears you and tells the manager he thinks you're a mystery shopper, that can cause the assignment to be made void and you won't get paid.

Discreet

It's also very important to be discreet when you take notes so that employees don't get suspicious. You can quickly take notes in a restroom or pretend you're texting a friend occasionally, if the situation allows. You'll be asked to remember employees' na.m.es, appearance, timing of service, etc. It's a lot to remember! You have to be pretty sneaky! That's why this job is often called "secret shopping."

It's important to remember that most places of business have cameras set up inside and outside their establishment, so if the mystery shop company is suspicious of the things you write in your report, they could easily contact the business and look through the video recordings and time sta.m.ps of when you said you visited their location. In other words, be honest.

If you accidentally forget to evaluate a particular item that you were required to, don't make up things in your report. Instead, immediately contact your scheduler and let him/her know what happened. You might not get paid for the assignment if the missing item was something really crucial, but they'll respect that you were honest and probably give you another chance.

Be Professional

Another important point I want to mention is that it's extremely important to behave yourself. While you're supposed to act like a "normal" customer, you are NOT to engage in a fight with an employee or make a scene if the service isn't to your standards. If you have a restaurant assignment, for example, you are allowed to order condiments or sauces on the side, but the mystery shop company won't want your order to be so bizarre that it calls attention to the staff. Many assignments will ask you to identify a manager, yet you're not to complain to the manager or demand anything out of the ordinary. If you are dining and drinking alcohol that is required for a particular assignment, only order what is required. NEVER get drunk or order beyond the requirement. You are working and expected to be professional at all times.

Be fair

Depending on what you write in your report, an employee could be rewarded or even fired for his/her behavior during your interaction with him/her. You need to be honest about what happened. The manager of the business will determine how to handle the staff, not you. In other words, you shouldn't write something in your report like, "This goon was so disrespectful that he should be fired!" You would simply write what the employee said or did and the business owner or manager will decide if it's an unacceptable offense or not.

In restaurant assignments, a common requirement is for you to record the timing of how long it took for food or drink items to be delivered after you ordered them. Please do NOT make those up! The timing is extremely important to the restaurant, which is why they are paying a mystery shop company to find out how their staff performed. I simply text what I've ordered after the server has walked away. All cell phones have a time stamp feature, but make sure yours does before doing this. When the food has been delivered and the server has walked away again, I text another message. Both messages will show a time stamp, which helps me when it's time for me to type up my report at home.

You Work For The Mystery Shop Company

Finally, NEVER contact a client directly. Your only communication should be with the mystery shop company. THEY will contact the client on your behalf. Technically, you work for the mystery shop company, not the client.

Now, I hope all of that didn't scare you away! It's a lot of fun and if free is your "jam", like me, you'll get a real kick out of it. You're helping companies get the information they need to do their very best for their customers. What you do truly matters.

WRITING YOUR REPORT

Your Words Matter

After you visit the location for your assignment, you will type up a report on the mystery shop company's website. Most companies will give you 24 hours to write up your report and submit it. The turnaround window is fairly quick because the store managers or restaurant owners want to be able to correct any problems found as fast as possible. Assignments will take about 15 minutes to 2 hours to write up once you get home, depending on the type of assignment and how detailed it has to be.

Often times, employees are given special awards if they are mentioned in a mystery shop report for providing exceptional service to you. The opposite is also true; an employee can be fired if you found him or her to be doing something truly awful or neglecting his duties to the harm of customers or himself. The business owners who will read your report will take your words very seriously, so it's extremely important to be honest and to choose your words carefully.

What You Write About

One misconception about mystery shopping is that a customer (you) can go into a store, generally observe what happens inside, and then write a report with opinions of whatever you think should have happened. That's not true. The client and the mystery shop company work together to identify what is most important and then create a detailed report that you need to fill out. For example, some questions you have to answer might be:

- Were you greeted within 60 seconds of your arrival?

- Were the glass windows clean and smudge-free?
- Was there debris on the floor throughout the store and in the restroom?
- Were you able to identify a manager? What was he/she doing?
- How many customers were in front of you when you got in line at the cash register?
- Was the cash register closed after every transaction?

There will be a series of detailed questions that you are given BEFORE you perform your assignment. That way, you know exactly which areas to observe and take notes on. You're not choosing random things to talk about in your report; you're reporting on exactly what happened in the specific areas the client wants to know about. You're not giving your opinion; you're writing an unbiased record of what you experienced. There will be times, usually in restaurant assignments, where you might be asked something like, "What could we have done to truly wow you during your visit?" That's when you can share your personal opinion. Unfortunately, not every company asks for your opinion, so just keep to the facts.

Grammar and Spelling

It's extremely important to be a good writer and follow the mystery shop company's writing guidelines perfectly. Pay special attention to how they want things written, because each company may emphasize particular things differently. For example, some companies allow you to write words like "don't" and "didn't", while other companies insist you be more precise by only writing "do not" and "did not." Your words matter and how you write your words matters.

As I mentioned earlier, some mystery shop companies will offer writing tutorials or even classes you can attend. They WANT you to write well, so they will often provide tips and tools so you can be successful. If you need extra help, ask for it.

I highly recommend you use the free Grammarly extension on Chrome. It does a great job of picking up spelling and grammatical errors. It's awesome. A simple technique to catch additional spelling and grammatical errors is to run your Word document through Spell-Check, although many mystery shop companies offer an internal Spell-Check of their own as you complete the written report. Reading your report out loud before hitting the submit button can also be helpful.

Spelling and punctuation matter, so if you need help, you can find all kinds of free writing guides online. A few I like are:

- www.Gra.m.marcheck.net
- www.Scribens.com
- www.VirtualwritingTutor.com

Editor

After you submit your written report online, an editor at the mystery shop company will go over your writing. If they're not happy with it, they'll ask for corrections. Since time is money, you'll want to avoid going back and forth in this editing process by simply writing a correct report the first time.

You need to be available by phone and/or email for the next 48 hours after you submit your report in case the editor needs to contact you with further questions. They may need you to email more details or contact them by phone to explain something they're not sure about in your report. If you plan on going on vacation after your assignment, let them know that ahead of time so they can expedite the editing process.

By the way, mystery shopping companies are always looking to hire great editors!

Your Grade

It's important to know that most companies have some kind of internal grading system to evaluate how well YOU performed the assignment. If they had to return your report for lots of edits or you missed certain requirements, they will notice and record that information. They usually share your score with you and give you feedback on how to improve. If you did a terrible job, they can refuse to reimburse you or pay you. So, don't do a terrible job! Remember, this is supposed to be fun and profitable! What you do reflects on the mystery shop company, so they want to help you and have you become a reliable shopper they can use over and over again. They have to please their client, so they want shoppers they can trust.

GETTING PAID

How Much Money Do You Want?

This is NOT a get-rich-scheme, but you can earn hundreds to thousands of dollars while also getting lots of free stuff all year long! If you live in a large city, there will be plenty of opportunities for assignments. If you live in a smaller town, the quantity of assignments may be limited unless you're willing to travel a little farther away from home. I used to be more willing to travel for assignments, but now I'm much more selective. There is usually as much work available as you're willing to do.

What you have to decide is whether or not a particular assignment is worth your time to do. If you're already going to see a movie, why not get paid to watch it and comment on the theater staff? If you're already going out for dinner, why not get paid to eat? I love those kinds of assignments, but if it's going to take me an hour to write an unusually long report to only earn a few dollars by going out of my way to some store I'd never want to visit, then I simply don't accept the assignment. Remember to calculate your travel time and writing time in your decision. Some assignments and companies pay very well…others, not so much. A good company will never force you to take an assignment you don't want to do. You get to decide. I love that!

Taxes

Another thing to consider when determining whether or not to accept an assignment is the tax you'll need to pay on the income you earn. At the end of the tax year, each mystery shop company you do work for will send you Independent Contractor documents for you to submit when you file your taxes. Here in the United States, it's called a W-9 form. If you earn less than $600 on assignments during the year, the companies generally won't send you any paperwork. You're not considered an employee, so you will be responsible to file your Independent Contractor income information. It's important to keep good records and be honest. I hope this doesn't sound scary or complicated. Even after all of that, mystery shopping is still very profitable and fun!

Payment

Mystery shop companies vary in how they choose to pay their shoppers. Most of them will simply mail you a check, while others prefer direct deposit into the bank account of your choosing. Some like the simplicity of PayPal. Once you have signed up with a company, be sure you are set up correctly in order to receive payment and reimbursements.

There are often two parts to payment after you complete an assignment: reimbursement and report payment. For example, if you are required to purchase a clothing item in a dress shop for $40, you might receive two checks in the mail: one for the $40 reimbursement and the other one for whatever the payment was to write up the report. That could be anywhere between $5 and $50, depending on how detailed and lengthy that assignment might be. Often times, the combined payment arrives as two separate checks because the mystery shop companies keep track of their accounts that way. Sometimes you'll receive it all in one lump sum. You'll also see this scenario when you dine in a restaurant. You'll receive one payment to reimburse for the food you bought and another payment to write up the report.

When you write up your report, you will be uploading copies of your receipts, so you will either need to use your cell phone to take a picture of them or else scan them into your computer to upload to the mystery shop company's website.

Here are some scenarios you might be wondering about.

You accept an assignment at a restaurant where you're allowed to spend $150 for dinner with a payment of $20 to write up a report.

What if you spend $164.97 for dinner? The company sends you the agreed upon $150 for dinner and $20 for the report.

What if you only spend $132.86 for dinner? The company sends you $132.86 for dinner and $20 for the report.

In other words, you will be given a maximum spending amount which is the amount you will be reimbursed UP TO. If you spend less than the maximum, you're reimbursed for that lower dollar amount.

Some companies will also reimburse you for valet or parking fees. Before you accept an assignment, make sure you completely understand the spending amounts and the form of payment.

Cash flow

Recognize that most assignments will ask you to use YOUR money with a promise for reimbursement. The good news is that you can also earn frequent flyer points on your credit cards when you use them for assignments. The bad news is that you need to be able to afford to spend the money and be patient for reimbursement, which can take as long as a month. On occasion, I've accepted assignments that required me to pay cash. If you can't afford to spend the money because it will put you in a cash-flow problem, simply don't accept the assignment.

It's important to keep records of all of your expenses and reimbursements, especially if you're going to accept a lot of assignments. A simple Excel spreadsheet works fine. If payment is taking a really long time, feel free to call or email the company. A few times my payments slipped through the cracks, but once I contacted the companies, they were quick to make amends. Don't get angry and throw a tantrum or they may not give you any more assignments.

If you have a copier, you can print out the assignment details and your written report. You can keep your receipts in a folder and then toss them once you have been paid and that year's tax season has passed. However you choose to organize your records, just be sure to do it! Remember to ONLY work with reputable mystery shop companies! If an assignment or company smells fishy to you, walk away.

Over the years, there have been assignments that didn't require me to use my own money. For example, I worked with a mystery shop company in Georgia, where I lived at the time, that would send me a gift certificate to pay for my meals. I would simply give the gift certificate to the waiter when the bill was to be paid. That was awesome, but kind of a rare scenario.

Records

It's important to be organized, especially if you do assignments for several different mystery shopping companies. Be sure to keep track of all of your mystery shop assignments so that you know what amount you are owed by the mystery shopping companies you do work for. Sometimes when they pay you, they identify the assignment and date, but sometimes you just receive a check with very little information on it.

If you ever have any questions about payment, don't hesitate to call the accounting department at the mystery shopping company. They will be happy to explain anything you need more information about.

When I keep records of my assignments, I simply use an Excel spreadsheet and include things like:

- Date of assignment
- Location of store/restaurant/etc.
- Scheduler name
- Confirmation # (if I have one)
- Reimbursement amount (if a purchase is required)
- Payment for written report
- Date paid
- Check number (if payment is received by check)

I also have a paper folder for each mystery shopping company where I keep the actual receipts from my purchases. As soon as that year's tax season is over, I throw them away.

SAMPLE REPORT

The following is a sample of what a written report might look like. Most companies have an online questionnaire that you fill out, which includes checking boxes of items in various categories and providing short commentary. Depending on the length of the report, this could take you anywhere from 15 minutes to 2 hours. The faster you are at typing and the better you are at grammar and spelling, the quicker you'll be able to complete the report.

Notice how detailed some of this information is. Each mystery shop company will inform you of what kind of writing and detail they require you to include in your report. Sometimes, the company only needs you to write two or three sentences. Sometimes, they ask for a very detailed, blow-by-blow account of everything that happened.

Phone Call:

I called The Restaurant at 11:15 a.m. on Thursday, December 5, 2013 by dialing 555-542-1866. The phone was answered after two rings by a professional female voice that said, "Thank you for calling The Restaurant." She then introduced herself as Janet and asked how she could help me. Her voice was clear and cheerful.

I asked Janet whether I needed to make reservations for that evening or could just walk in. She told me that they did not accept reservations for parties of less than 12 people. She then asked me how many people there were in my party and I told her it would just be two of us.

Janet then informed me that parties of two were normally seated quickly. She added that seating would also be available at the bar. I then asked about nearby parking and Janet gave me the cross streets for the nearest parking garage. She indicated that tickets could be validated, further explaining that we would not have to pay for parking.

I thanked Janet for the information, and she closed with, "My pleasure." Her tone was friendly and pleasant. Janet was helpful and friendly during the call.

Hostess:

My guest and I entered the restaurant at 6:30 p.m. on Saturday, December 7, 2013. Host #1 (Female - 5'4", straight, blonde hair) was talking to the Maître d' (Male - 6'2" short, brown hair), but they immediately ended their conversation and acknowledged me with friendly eye contact and smiles. Host #2 (Female - 5'9", short, black hair) greeted us with "Table for two?" She spoke in a polite tone of voice and made direct eye contact with us, but she did not smile. I confirmed that it was just the two of us and host #2 gathered two menus and handed them to host #1.

Host #1 then invited us to follow her to a table. She engaged me in light conversation, turning around occasionally as she spoke. She said, "I love your cute scarf! Where did you get it?" When we reached the table, she waited for us to be seated and then handed us menus. She then told us to enjoy our dinner and left the table. She did not pull out our chairs for us. The table was set for 2 people, so she did not have to remove any unused table settings.

The hostess podium was staffed throughout the visit. The hosts greeted guests immediately and seemed to seat them in similar manner experienced by me and my guest.

As my guest and I left the restaurant at 8:40 p.m., host #1 nodded towards us. She smiled and cheerfully said, "Goodbye! Have a good evening!" She smiled and made good eye contact.

Manager:

During the evaluation, I observed the manager (Male - 5'7", blonde hair, goatee) interacting with the staff members near the podium and on the service floor. He was also seen assisting servers and serving guests at tables. The manager visited my table at 8:04 p.m., just after I had received my dessert. He smiled at us, made eye contact, and said "How is everything?" He spoke in a friendly tone of voice. I told him that everything was fine.

The manager then asked if there was anything that he could get for us, and he offered us refills. He smiled at us as he walked past us later that evening. He was carrying empty plates to the kitchen. The manager was seen interacting with two tables, and he seemed upbeat when engaging all guests. He was dressed professionally and was very polite.

When I left the restaurant at the end of my meal, both the manager and the Maître d' smiled and thanked me for coming. They both said, "Have a good night!" and "Goodbye!"

Bar:

I took a seat at the bar at 6:30 p.m. There were four other guests at the bar. Two of the guests appeared to be sharing an appetizer. Barnet (name on check) greeted me immediately with, "Hi. How are you doing?" He smiled, made eye contact with me, and used a friendly tone of voice. Barnet put a napkin in front of me and asked if I wanted to see the drink menu. I said that I did, and he put the menu in front of me. The menu was clean. I did not detect any errors on the menu.

After perusing the menu, I ordered a gin and tonic. Barnet quickly prepared the drink, checking whether I wanted lemon or lime as a garnish. I requested a sprig of mint and he set it down in front of me within one minute. He used an ice scoop when preparing the drink, and I noted that he did not handle the glass by the rim. He then asked if I wanted to see the food menu and I agreed.

I looked at the menu for some time and then asked Barnet if the menu was new. He confirmed that it was and pointed out some of the new additions to the menu. He also told me which dishes were popular amongst the regulars and recommended a couple of dishes.

Barnet noticed that my drink was getting low and offered to refill it for me. I explained that I was going to have dinner and didn't want to fill up on drinks. He smiled and asked if I wanted him to offer suggestions on food items. I said yes and asked him to explain some of the appetizer selections.

Barnet recommended the chicken sliders and described how they were prepared. I asked him what his favorite entrée was, and he said the tri-tip with rice was delicious. I asked him if the Asian chicken skewers were spicy and he said yes.

Barnet was very knowledgeable about the menu and talked enthusiastically about the food.

Barnet did not eat any food while I was seated at the bar. I could see him from my table during my meal and did not observe him eating then either.

Every now and then, Barnet would sip some bottled water, but that was all I ever saw him drink. He was professional and kept busy all night, helping guests and the other bartenders that joined him later on.

Barnet kept the bar area very clean. It wasn't too busy, so he was able to spend quite a bit of time cleaning and wiping the counter down. Dirty glasses and bottles were removed from the bar area within three minutes. There were no spills, but he removed napkins and straws from the bar counter quickly. Barnet was organized and neat.

I asked Barnet if he served blender drinks like Pina coladas. Barnet said yes and assured me that they were delicious. Instead, I asked for a gin and tonic and he asked if I wanted premium gin. Barnet made some suggestions and I chose one.

At 6:37 p.m., Barnet passed by and asked if I wanted a glass of water. I accepted. He served the water with a lemon wheel. At 6:43 p.m., my guest met me at the bar. Barnet greeted her in a friendly manner as he set a drink menu down in front of her. She told him that she was fine, and he offered her water. Noting that my drink was low, he then offered me a refill. I declined and asked for the check, commenting that we were heading to the dining room for dinner.

Barnet immediately printed out a check for me. He set it on the bar top, and I placed a $10 bill on the check. One minute 16 seconds later, he collected the cash, opened the cash drawer, placed the cash inside, took out some change, and then closed the drawer. He handed me $5.25 in change, along with an itemized receipt. Barnet thanked me as he handed me my change, making direct eye contact with me as he did so. I placed a tip on the bar top.

As my guest and I left the bar at 6:45 p.m., Barnet smiled at us, made eye contact, and waved. He was at the other end of the bar, wiping down the counter. Barnet was neat and clean in appearance. He was friendly and professional, and he seemed to engage guests warmly at the bar. He did not touch his face, hair, or mouth. I did not see him eating during the visit, although he occasionally took sips from a bottle of Dasani water.

Pours were a consistent size. Glassware was properly handled, and an ice scoop was used when required. Garnishes were appropriate. I noticed that Barnet washed the shaker between preparing drinks for guests and servers. Drinks for the dining room were always accompanied by tickets. The wooden bar top was wiped clean and did not have any dirty dishes or glassware on it. The shelves behind the bar were neatly stocked with various bottles of liquor. The preparation area behind the bar was neat and well organized.

The cash drawer remained closed at all times when it was not in use. I did not observe any mishandling of money.

6:43 p.m. Gin and Tonic ordered, served. Up sell suggested. Entered into POS with several hand strokes. No payment requested. Later paid with cash.

6:45 p.m. 1 mix drink ordered. Tequila suggested. Drink served, credit card given, tab offered and accepted. Entered into POS with several hand strokes, tab started.

6:47 p.m. 1 Budweiser ordered, served. No up sale. Entered into POS with several hand strokes. Tab offered and declined. Bill paid with cash. Tip paid.

6:48 p.m. 1 Budweiser ordered, served. No up sell. Entered into POS with several hand strokes. Guest still seated at bar when I left to my dining table. No payment had been requested.

Server:

One minute after my guest and I were seated, Mia (name on check) approached the table at 6:49 p.m. She smiled, made eye contact, offered a friendly "Hello ladies." Mia then told us that she would be our server for the evening.

Mia asked if it was our first time at the restaurant. I told her that it was my guest's first time, adding that I had not been to the restaurant in some time. Mia welcomed me back and said that she was happy that I had brought my guest. She then explained the shared concept and told us that dishes were brought out as they were prepared. She then said she would give us a few minutes to look over the menu. Mia was friendly and polite. She greeted us warmly and made us feel welcome immediately.

At 6:50 p.m. Mia returned and asked if we wanted to order drinks. I asked for water with no ice and my guest asked for ice water. She asked whether we wanted bottled water or tap water and I said tap water was fine. Mia asked me if I would be interested in a specialty cocktail and recommended the wine-by-glass specials. I ordered a gin and tonic for me and my guest. Mia delivered the water within two minutes, at approximately 6:54 p.m. She checked to see if we were ready to order, but I asked for more time.

At 6:57 p.m., my guest and I put down our menus and Mia approached us right away. She asked us if we had any questions and I told her that I was trying to decide between the ravioli and the pasta of the day. She helped me decide between the two, commenting on the ingredients, portion size, and asking me some questions to determine my preferences. I then ordered the ravioli. I also ordered Crab Pad Thai as an entrée. My guest ordered the Sea Bass and substituted a side dish.

Mia was very helpful all night with the menu. She made helpful recommendations and made the food sound delicious. I was worried about spicy dishes, so Mia successfully steered me away from certain dishes. Mia waited for me and my guest to decide what we wanted and then when we were ready, she was quickly available. My guest and I ordered a steak appetizer, so Mia asked how we would like the steak cooked. I said, "Medium well," and she said, "Great!"

After we ordered our food, Mia left and then quickly returned with proper utensils and small plates for our starter course. She was very attentive and fast. I ordered ravioli and asked if I could have an extra side of Alfredo sauce. Mia said "Of course! It's delicious!" When Mia delivered my entrée, she brought a small bowl of Alfredo sauce on the side. She remembered my special request and served it on a small dish.

At 7:19 p.m., Mia delivered our entrees. She stopped by three minutes later to ask us how we were enjoying our dishes. I told her that it was good. When we were done with the entrees, Mia asked if she could remove our dishes. She cleared them away at 7:52 p.m. She then asked if we wanted to order dessert and quickly got some menus for us when I said that we did.

Mia was very attentive all night long. We never had to wait for her to walk by our table. She kept watch on the timing and was very professional. Her assistant was Jose (Male, Hispanic, 5'4", short, black hair).

Jose was very polite and attentive all evening. He always asked us if we were finished eating a particular course before he cleared the dishes from the table. Jose brought new utensils and plates before our appetizers were delivered, as well as our entrees and desserts. Dishes and utensils were cleared quickly and quietly. The table was wiped of crumbs after our appetizers and entrees. The table was kept clean and professional. Jose worked quickly and quietly.

I requested the check at 8:15 p.m. Mia delivered an itemized check one minute later at 8:16 p.m. The check was accurate and clean. She picked up my credit card at 8:18 P.M. and returned with receipts at 8:13 p.m.

Mia made eye contact and smiled at us all night long. She politely said, "Thank you, ladies." She was both friendly and professional throughout the meal. We got up to leave the table at 8:30 p.m.

Food:

I ordered the Steak Kabob appetizer to share with my guest. It was served hot and on 3 skewers. The meat was cooked medium well, as ordered. The presentation was very appetizing with the Steak Kabob on a bed of rice pilaf and a parsley garnish.

The appetizer was tasty and very satisfying. It was worth the price and very fresh. The quality was very good and high. The portion size was perfect for 2 people to share as an appetizer. It was above average and worth the value.

The cheese ravioli was served hot. The platter contained four large ravioli on a bed of marinara sauce. The ravioli was stuffed with a creamy cheese filling and sprinkled with fresh parmesan cheese. The serving size was generous for an entrée because the ravioli sections were very large and fat. The dish met expectations and was delicious and was an excellent value.

The quality was very high, and the ingredients were fresh. A small house salad was also on the platter, surprising me as an extra. The presentation was artistic with a decorative swirl of Alfredo on the platter. I asked for a side of Alfredo sauce, which was delivered along with the entrée.

The Monkey Pie dessert was as described by the server. The pastries were buttery and soft with a bronzed outer layer. It was served warm with a scoop of chilled vanilla ice cream. and candied nuts. The dessert was attractively presented. It was the perfect size for one guest. This dessert surpassed expectations because it was unique and full of flavor. The size was appropriate for one guest after a big dinner. The price was reasonable and appropriate. The dish was above average and a good value.

The chocolate cupcake was served at room temperature on a plate sprinkled with powdered sugar. It was small, but very rich. It was attractively presented with a dollop of cream. and fresh strawberries. The dessert met expectations. The price was reasonable. It was an average value because it wasn't anything unusual.

I ordered a Chardonnay at the table and it was quickly delivered by Mia with a smile. The glass was room temperature and attractively shaped. The portion size was appropriate for the price. It was tasty and flavorful. It was presented on a special tray.

Restaurant Facility:

The lighting in the restaurant was a bit dark so I used my cell phone to provide extra light to read the menu. There was a candle in a small votive on my table, adding a nice ambiance.

The music was instrumental and played softly in the background, so as not to distract guests. It was nice. The temperature in the restaurant was perfect. I did not need to wear my jacket and was comfortable. The sidewalk surrounding the restaurant was free of debris and spills. The windows appeared clean. The entrance door was in good condition. The entrance was free of debris.

The foyer area was clean with minimal debris visible on the carpet. The podium directly in front of the entrance was clean and uncluttered. The seating arrangements were good. Chairs were all sturdy and in good condition. The tables were also well maintained and polished. There was plenty of space between the tables and guests and staff members could comfortably walk through.

The table settings were complete. They included clean silverware and white napkins. The china was free of defects. The glassware was also in good condition. The menus were professional in appearance and content, and they were easy to read. The text was not too small.

I visited the women's restroom at 6:55 p.m. It was free of odors, and fully stocked with toilet paper, soap and towels. The restroom was attractive and modern. All of the surfaces and fixtures were clean. The waste bin had plenty of room in it for more trash. My guest visited the restroom at 7:58 p.m. She found it in a similar condition.

The sidewalk outside the restaurant was clean and free of debris. The front doors were clean and attractive. There were no smudges, nor fingerprints. The entryway was clean and appeared recently swept. The front windows were also clean and smudge-free. The entranceway just outside the restaurant was clean and decorated for Christmas.

This is a lovely restaurant with excellent service and delicious food. The staff made me feel like a wanted customer and that I was their top priority. Everyone was extremely attentive. The staff was very cheerful and busy all night. They appeared to work as a team. and enjoy their place of work.

As I left the restaurant at the end of the evening, the bus boy, server, and manager all said good-bye and thanked me for coming. Their salutations were sincere and expressed with a smile.

I would definitely return to this restaurant and bring friends! The price is reasonable and comparable to other restaurants of this style. Some of the dishes were very unique and made this restaurant stand out.

The staff appeared to be very well trained and worked nicely together. They had good attitudes and appeared to enjoy working at the restaurant. They were extremely nice and attentive. I asked for recommendations by the bartender and the server. They knew the menu well and excitedly suggested their favorites. I felt that the staff valued my business and wanted to make sure I was satisfied. Their interest and help appeared sincere. All staff members were very polite and pleasant.

THE LIST OF COMPANIES FROM A TO Z

Here is a fairly comprehensive list of Mystery Shopping Companies. There are also Merchandising companies listed, as these services often go hand-in-hand. Merchandising companies pay you to stock their company's products in stores. It's different from mystery shopping companies, but because a lot of mystery shoppers tend to like those kinds of assignments too, they're included in the list below.

Not all companies accept shoppers in all areas, so read the application pages to see if you are in an eligible location. Another place you can find good companies is www.volition.com/mystery.html

Mystery shopping companies come and go over the years, so please accept my apology if you discover any errors on this list. I try to keep it updated, but things change quickly in this industry.

Have fun!

-A-
ABA Quality Monitoring Ltd (UK)
www.aba.co.uk/

About Face Corp.
www.aboutfacecorp.com

Absolute Advantedge
www.absoluteadvantedge.com/

Accent Merchandising International (A.M.I)
www.accentmerchandising.com/

Acorn (UK)
www.acornmysteryshop.com

Acosta Sales and Marketing
www.acosta.com

ACE™ Mystery Shopping or Associate Consumer Evaluations
www.acemysteryshopping.com

ActionLink
www.actionlink.biz

ACRA, Inc.
www.secretshopacra.com

ActionPlus Service
www.actionplusservice.com/

A Closer Look
www.a-closer-look.com

Action Research Group
www.actionresearchgroup.org

A Customer's Point of View
www.acpview.com

Advanced Feedback
advancedfeedback.com

Advanced Phone Ups Inc.
phoneups.com

Advanced Retail Merchandising (ARM)
www.arm-retail.com/

Advantage Business Services
cwj32901@aol.com

Advantage Sales & Marketing
boyd.stevens@asmcanada.com

Advisor Marketing

www.advisorsmarketing.com/

Advisory Group, Inc.
kassoff@advisorygroupinc.com

Affinity Market Research
www.affinitymarketresearch.com

AIM Field Service
www.patsaim.com

All Shop Group
www.allshopgroup.com/
email: susan@allshopgroup.com

All State Market Solutions
https://www.allstatemarketsolutions.com/

ALCOPS - Allied Corporate Protective Service
www.alcops.com

All-Star Customer Service
www.mysteryshoppingexperts.com

Aloha Solutions
www.alohasolutions.net
alohasolutions@carolina.rr.com OR call at 704-989-4709

A&A Merchandising Ltd.
www.aa.m.erch.com/

A&M Business Services, Inc.
www.a.m.bussvcs.com

American Marketing Service
2690 S. White - Suite 80
San Jose, CA 95148
Phone: 408-239-1002
Fax: 408-238-2618
E-mail: pcottle@a.m.ericanmarketing.com

Amusement Advantage (Entertainment Venues)
www.a.m.usementadvantage.com

An Eye for Detail

www.aneyefordetailconsulting.com/

Ann Michaels & Associates, Ltd.
www.sassieshop.com/2annmichaels/

Anonymous Insights
www.a-insights.com

Anonymous Shoppers & Assessments of Pittsburgh
www.asapittsburgh.com

Apartment Shoppe
www.apartmentmysteryshopper.com

A-Plus Shopping
630-898-6268 OR Jenkins_karen@msn.com

AQ Services International
www.aq-services.com

ARC Research
www.arcresearch.com

Ardent Services
www.ardentservices.com

Ascent Research Associates, LLC
www.ascentresearch.com

Ask Arizona / West Group Research
www.westgroupresearch.com

Ask Southern California
www.asksocal.com/

Assure Quality Systems (ASQ)
aqsshopper@bellsouth.net

A Step Above Service Evaluations
www.serviceevaluations.com

Athena Research Group, Inc.
www.athena.m.arketresearch.com

Ath Power
www.athpower.com

www.athpoweronline.com/shoppers/LoginShopper.php

A Top Shop
www.atopshop.com/services.htm

A Total Resource Group (No website)
936 East 12th Ave
Denver, CO, US
303-813-0000
totalresourcegrp@aol.com

At Random Communications
www.arllc.com

At Your Service Marketing
www.aysm.com

Auditor Service (in Spanish)
www.auditorservice.com

Automotive Insights
www.automotiveinsights.com

-B-
Bank Atlantic
www.sassieshop.com/2bankatlantic/shoppers/LoginShopper.php

Bare Associates International (BAI)
www.baiservices.com/
www.baidata.com/shoppers/LoginShopper.php

BAI Hotel Evaluators
users.pandora.be/baiservices/

Baird Consulting
www.baird-consulting.com/
https://baird-consulting.clientsmart.com/
Barry Leeds & Associates
www.barryleedsassoc.com/

B. Business Solutions, Inc.
www.bizshoptalk.com/
shopper.BusinessSolutions.archondev.com

Benchmark Collaborative
www.sassieshop.com/2benchmark/shoppers/LoginShopper.php

Best Mark
https://www.bestmark.com/

Bevinco
www.bevinco.com/

Beyond Hello
https://www.beyondhello.com/secure/index.htm
www.hellomirror.com/shoppers/LoginShopper.php

Beyond Marketing Group
beyondmarketinggroup.com/

Best Market Audits, Inc. (BMA)
www.mystery-shopping.com

BMI (Mystery Shopper USA)
www.bmiltd.com/index.html

Brann National Retail Services
www.nationalretailservices.com

Business Evaluation Services
www.mysteryshopperservices.com

Business Insights Group
www.businessinsights.com/

Business Research Group
www.brgus.com/

Business Resources
www.bizpublications.com/

Buyers Choice
www.byerschoiceinc.com/

-C-
California Marketing Specialists
www.sassieshop.com/2california.m.arketing/shoppers/LoginShopper.php

Campaigners, Inc.
www.ca.m.paigners.com/

Campbell Edgar
www.retailcareers.com

Campus Consulting Mystery Shopping Service
www.shopaudits.com

Capstone Research
www.capstoneresearch.com/
www.sassieshop.com/2capstoneresearch/shoppers/LoginShopper.php

C-Chex (NY only)
www.c-chex.com

Certified Marketing Research Services
certifiedmarketingresearch.com/fieldworkeraccess.asp

Certified Reports Inc. (movie checks only)
www.certifiedreports.com

Channel Watch
www.channelwatch.net/

Check Mark
www.checkmarkinc.com

CheckUp Marketing
https://www.checkup.m.arketing.com

Chuck Latham Associates, Inc.
www.clareps.com/

Circle of Service
www.circle-of-service.com/

Cirrus Marketing Consultants
www.cirrusmktg.com
www.sassieshop.com/2cirrus

CKA Group
https://www.ckagroup.com

Classic Demos, Inc.

www.classicdemos.com/

Clear Evaluations
www.sassieshop.com/2clearevals/shoppers/LoginShopper.php

Client First Associates
www.cf-associates.com/

Concept Merchandising (PIMMS)
www.conceptmerchandising.com/

Confero
www.conferoinc.com/
www.sassieshop.com/2confero/shoppers/LoginShopper.php

Consumer Connections
consumerconnection.net/

Consumer Critique
www.consumercritique.com

Consumer Direct
www.customerdirect.com/

Consumer Eye
https://consumereye.clientsmart.com/index.php

Consumer Impressions
consumerimpressions.com

Consumer Impact Marketing, Ltd.
www.consumerimpact.com

Consumer Impressions
consumerimpressions.com/

Consumer Opinion (DO NOT ACCEPT UNSOLICITED)
www.cosvc.com/register.html

Consumer Perceptions Inc.
www.consumer-perceptions.com/
Kim Edwards, General Manager
Email kim@consumer-perceptions.com OR Call 1.800.692.3454

Consumer Research Group

www.crg2000.com/ProShoppers.htm

Continental Sales and Service, Inc.
www.homecenterservice.com/

Corporate Research Group (Canada Only)
www.crgms.com/general.cfm

Corporate Research International
www.mysteryshops.com

Corporate Risk Solutions
www.losspreventiongroup.net
www.sassieshop.com/2crs/shoppers/LoginShopper.php

Count On Us
www.ucountonus.com

Courtesy Counts—now merged with Ath Power

Coyle Hospitality Group
www.coylehospitality.com

Creative Image Associates
www.creativeimage.net/MysteryShoppers.aspx

Creative Marketing Concepts (apt shops east coast)
www.getcreativemarketing.com

Creative Restaurant Solutions
www.creativerestaurantsolutions.com
email: CRS_MRB@comcast.net

Cross Financial Group
crossfinancial.com

Crossmark
www.crossmark.com/

CRS/Lawrence Service
www.crslawrence.com/

CSD Assessments
www.csdassessments.com/

Customer 1st

customer-1st.com/shopper/default.asp
customer-1st.com/shopper/shopperlogin.asp

Customer Perspectives
www.customerperspectives.com
email: info@customerperspectives.com

Customer Point of View
www.mystery-shopper-business.com/restaurant-mystery-shopping
Email: cpvevals@earthlink.net

Customer Service Consultants
Maggie Setler
RR #2, Box 261-J - Kistler Dr
Export, PA 15632
(724) 327-7191
mjscgs@aol.com

Customer Service Experts
www.customerserviceexperts.com/
www.sassieshop.com/2shopcse/shoppers/LoginShopper.php

Customer Service Perceptions (registration fee)
csperceptions.com

Customer Service Profiles
www.csprofiles.com

Customer Service Solutions
www.mysteryshopusa.com

CustomeriZe
www.customerize.com/
www.sassieshop.com/2customerize/shoppers/LoginShopper.php

Customer Research Group
crg2000.com

-D-
DataQuest
www.dataquestonline.com

Datatron

www.usd-datatron.com/mystery_shopper.htm

David Sparks and Associates
www.sparksresearch.com

Deception Control, Inc.
www.deception.com

Devon Hill Associates
www.devonhillassociates.com
email: barbara@devonhillassociates.com

Devrew Merchandising (Canada)
www.devrew.com/

Diversified Corporate Solutions, Inc.
shopper.divcorp.com

Division21
www.division21.com

Douglas Stafford (UK based)
www.douglasstafford.com

Draude Marketing
www.sassieshop.com/2draude/shoppers/LoginShopper.norm.php

DSG Associates
www.dsgai.com

Dynamic Advantage
shops.dyna.m.ic-advantage.com

Dynamic Service Group
www.dyna.m.icservicegroup.com/

eDigitalResearch (UK)
www.edigitalresearch.com/eMysteryShopper/becomeanemysteryshopper.htm

-E-
Ellis Property Management Services
www.ep.m.sonline.com

Evaluation Systems for Personnel (ESP)
www.espshop.com

Examine Your Practice, Inc.
www.exa.m.ineyourpractice.com

Excel Shopping and Consulting
www.excelshoppingandconsulting.com

Expert Shopping Professionals
www.sassieshop.com/2esp/shoppers/LoginShopper.php

Extra Eyes Nationwide
www.extraeyes.net

Eye On Retail Merchandising
www.eyeonretail.com/

Eyes R Us, Inc.
www.eyesrusinc.com

-F-
Feedback Plus
shop.feedbackplus.com/

Field Facts Worldwide (UK, FR, GER)
www.fieldfacts.com

Field Marketing, Inc.
www.fieldmktg.com/

Fieldnet Mystery Shoppers (AU)
www.fieldnet.com.au/index.asp

First Glance
FirstGlanceInc@msn.com

Focus On Service, LLC
www.focusonservice.net

Franchise Compliance
www.franchisecompliance.com/
www.sassieshop.com/2franchisecompliance/shoppers/LoginShopper.php

Freeman Group Solutions
shopper.freemangroupsolutions.com

Frontline Shoppers
www.frontlineshoppers.com

Full Scope Mystery Shopping
www.fullscopemysteryshopping.com

FYI Video Shops (registration fee)
www.fyivideoshops.com

-G-
Game Film Consultants
www.ga.m.efilmconsultants.com/

Gates & Associates
g.associates@att.net

GAPbuster
www.gapbuster.com
www.xec.gapbuster.com/

Global Compliance Services
https://www.gcsresearch.com/applicationprocess.asp

Golden Resources Marketing Group
members.aol.com/cgr315/index.html
PO Box 71314
Marietta, GA 30007-1314

Goodwin & Associates
www.mysteryshopperprogra.m..com/msp

Grantham., Orilio & Associates (GOAShoppers)
4490 Fanuel St. Suite #222
San Diego, CA 92109
1-800-711-7776

Graymark Security Group
www.graymarksecurity.com

Green & Associates (now merged with Speedmark)

Greet America Mystery Shopping (registration fee)
www.ga-mysteryshopper.com

Guest Check
www.theguestcheck.com/

Guest Reflections
www.sassieshop.com/2guestreflections/shoppers/LoginShopper.php

-H-
Harris Teeter
www.sassieshop.com/2harristeeter/index.norm.php

Hausernet (Mail Advertisement Tracking Agent)
www.hausernet.com/newpage6.htm

Herron Research (mostly market research panels)
www.herron-research.com

Hidden Concepts, Inc.
www.hiddenconcepts.com/

Hilli Dunlap (use caution, as this company has had financial problems)
www.sassieshop.com/2hillidunlap/

Hindsight (also has a paid blasting service)
hndsight.com/

Hoed Holdings Pty Ltd (Austrailasia)
www.hoedholdings.com.au/hoed/

Hoffmann & Forcher Marketing Research (Austria)
www.hoffmannforcher.at/

Howard Services
www.howardservices.com/

HR & Associates, Inc.
www.hrandassociates.com

HR Options Retail Merchandising Services
www.hroptions.com/

-I-
ICC/Decision Services
https://www2.iccds.com/fr/frlogin.cfm

ICU
www.icuassociates.com
shopper.icuassociates.com/

Imaginus, Inc.
www.imaginusinc.com

Imedgexperts
www.imedgexperts.com

iMyst
www.imyst.com/login

Informa Research Services, Inc.
www.informa.m.ysteryshop.com/login.cfm

Infotel (can only view shops in specified zip code zones)
www.infotelinc.com

Inland Retail Services
www.inlandretailservices.com

The Insight Group (looking for hospitality experience)
www.theinsightgroupintl.com

Instant Reply
www.mysteryshopservices.com/

Insula Research, Inc.
www.InsulaResearch.com
shopper.insularesearch.archondev.com/InsulaResearch/Shoppers.nsf

Integrity Auditing Services
www.integrity-auditing.com

Intellishop
insite.intelli-shop.com/shoppers/LoginShopper.php

International Hospitality Check
www.sassieshop.com/2ihc/shoppers/LoginShopper.php

International Service Check
www.internationalservicecheck.com
www.multisearchweb.com/login.jsp

Ipsos-Insight
www.ipsos-na.com
www.sassieshop.com/2ipsos/shoppers/LoginShopper.php

i-Spy
ispy4u.net/shoppers.htm

ITS Incognito
www.itsincognito.com

-J-
Jancyn
www.jancyn.com/
shoppers.jancyn.com

JC & Associates
www.jcandassociates.com

J.E. Lowery Professional Services Corporation
members.hometown.aol.com/investigator1950/myhomepage/index.html

JKS Inc.
www.jksinc.com

JM Ridgway
www.jmridgway.com/
www.sassieshop.com/2JMRidgway/shoppers/LoginShopper.php

-K-
Kaiz Hospitalty Services
www.kaizconsult.com

Karandy and Associates
Email: jkarandy@aol.com

Ken-Rich Retail Group
www.ken-rich.com

Keystone Marketing
www.keystone2000.com

Kinesis- CEM
www.kinesis-cem.com
shopper.kinesis-cem.com

KLD Research
www.kldresearch.com

-L-
Lasting Impressions
www.mystery-shop.net

LeBlanc & Associates
www.mleblanc.com

Locksley Group
LGLGROUP@aol.com

LRA Worldwide Inc.
www.lraworldwide.com/
www.sassieshop.com/2LRA/shoppers/LoginShopper.php

-M-
Maritz
https://www.virtuoso.maritzresearch.com/profile/default.asp

Marketing Endeavors
www.marketingendeavors.biz/
www.sassieshop.com/2me/shoppers/LoginShopper.php

Market Research Dallas
marketresearchdallas.com

Marketing Systems Unlimited
www.msultd.com

Market Trends
www.sassieshop.com/2markettrends/

Market Viewpoint
www.marketviewpoint.com

Mars Research
www.marsresearch.com
Email: joyceg@marsresearch.com

Measure Consumer Perspectives
measurecp.com
www.sassieshop.com/2msr

Melinda Brody (apartment shops)
www.melindabrody.com

Mercantile Systems & Surveys
www.sassieshop.com/2mercsurveys/shoppers/LoginShopper.norm.php

Merchandise Concepts
www.merchandiseconcepts.com

Mike's Mystery Shopping Service
www.angelfire.com/pa/mystershopper/Home
www.angelfire.com/pa/mystershopper/employment

Mintel
www.mintel.com
shopper.mintel.com

Michelson & Associates, Inc (now merged with Service Evaluation Concepts)

Mosaic InfoForce
www.mosaic-infoforce.com

Mystery Diners, Inc.
www.mysterydinersinc.com/
diners.mysterydinersinc.com/

Mystery Guest
www.mysteryguestinc.com

Mystery Shopper Pros
www.mysteryshopperpros.com/
shopper.mysteryshopperpros.com/

Mystery Shoppers
www.sassieshop.com/2mysteryshoppers/

Mystery Shoppers, Inc.
www.mysteryshopinc.com
www.sassieshop.com/2mysteryshopinc/shoppers/LoginShopper.php

Mystique Shopper, LLC
www.mystiqueshopper.com
www.sassieshop.com/2mystique/shoppers/LoginShopper.php

-N-
National In-Store
www.nationalinstore.com

National Shopping Service
www.nationalshoppingservice.com

National Shopping Service Network
www.mysteryshopper.net

Nationwide Services Group
www.nationwidesg.com
www.sassieshop.com/2nis/shoppers/LoginShopper.norm.php

Nsite
https://www.nsiteinc.com

NWLPC (NW Loss Prevention Consultants)
shoppers.nwlpc.com/

-O-
OA Hospitality
www.sassieshop.com/2goa/shoppers/LoginShopper.php

-P-
Pacific Research Group
www.pacificresearchgroup.com/
65.119.21.227/shoppers2/login.asp

Peak Techniques, Inc. (PTI)
www.peaktechniques.com/
shopper.pti.archondev.com/

People Plus
www.mapnetwork.net/peopleplus.html

Perception Strategies
www.perstrat.com

Perfect Performance
Email: perfectperform@aol.com

The Performance Edge
www.pedge.com

Person To Person Quality
persontopersonquality.com

Pinkerton
www.ci-pinkerton.com/

Phantom Shoppers
www.sassieshop.com/2phantom/

Phantom Shopping
www.phantomshopping.com

PhoneSmart
www.phone-smart.info
Email: tron@phone-smart.net

Premier Service
www.premierservice.ca

Primo Solutions LLC
www.primosolutionsllc.com
shopper.primosolutionsllc.com

Professional Review
www.sassieshop.com/2proreview/shoppers/LoginShopper.php

Promotion Network, Inc
www.promotionnetworkinc.com

PulseBack
www.pulseback.com

-Q-
QSI Specialists
www.qsispecialists.com

Quality Assessments Mystery Shoppers
www.qa.m.s.com

Quality Assurance Consulting
www.qacinc.com/

Quality Check Undercover Shoppers (registration fee)
https://www.undercovershoppers.com/Shopper_Page.html

Quality Marketing Group
www.qmgrp.com

Quality Service Control
www.sassieshop.com/2qsc/shoppers/LoginShopper.php

Quality Shopper
www.qualityshopper.org

Quality Works Associates
www.qualityworks.com

Quinn Marketing and Communications
www.quinnmc.com
www.sassieshop.com/2quinn/index.norm.php

Quest for the Best
www.questforbest.com
shopper.questforbest.com

-R-
Reality Check Mystery Shoppers
www.rcmysteryshopper.com/
www.sassieshop.com/2rcms/shoppers/LoginShopper.php

Reflections MS
www.reflectionsms.com

Regal Hospitality
shopper.regalhg.com/

Rentrack Corp.
https://ms.rentrak.com

Restaurant Cops
www.restaurant-cops.com/
shopper.restaurant-cops.com

Restaurant Evaluators.com
www.restaurantevaluators.com

Retail Eyes
www.retaileyes.com

Retail Track
www.retailtrack.com

Rickie Kruh Research & Marketing Group
Email: rkrmg@aol.com

Ritter Associates
www.ritterassociates.com

Roberte Verifications
www.roberteverifications.com

Roper NOP
www.cybershoppersonline.com

-S-
Satisfaction Services
www.satisfactionservicesinc.com

Second To None
www.second-to-none.com
evaluator2.second-to-none.com/evaluator

Secret Mystery Shopping
www.secretmysteryshopping.info

Secret Shop Communicators
www.sscomminc.com
Emailed: fhsecretshop@prodigy.ne

Secret Shopper
www.secretshopper.com

The Secret Shopper Company
secretshoppercompany.com

Secret Shopping Services
www.sassieshop.com/2sss

Sensors Quality Management
www.sqm.ca

Sensus
www.sensusresearch.com/

Sentry Marketing Group, LLC
www.sentrymarketinggroup.com
shopper.sentrymarketinggroup.com

The Sentry Marketing Group
apply.sentrymarketing.com/

Service Advantage International
www.servad.com
shopper.servad.com/

Service Alliance, Inc.
www.serviceallianceinc.com
www.sassieshop.com/2servicealliance

Service Check
www.servicecheck.com
www.servicecheckreport.com/shoppers/LoginShopper.php

Service Connections
www.serviceconnectionsinc.com

Service Evaluations
Email: bcline@service-evaluations.com

Service Evaluation Concepts
www.serviceevaluation.com/

Service Excellence Group
www.serviceexcellencegroup.com/
www.sassieshop.com/2servicex/shoppers/LoginShopper.php

Service Impressions
www.sassieshop.com/2serviceimpressions/

Service Intelligence
www.secretshopnet.com/

Service Performance
www.sassieshop.com/2serviceperformance/

Service Probe
www.pwgroup.com
www.marniepehrson.com

Service Quality
www.service-quality.com

Service Research Corporation
www.serviceresearch.com
shopper.serviceresearch.com

Service Research Group
www.serviceresearchgroup.com
Email: RFP@serviceresearchgroup.com

Service Savvy
www.sassieshop.com/2servicesavvy/shoppers/LoginShopper.php

ServiceSense
www.servicesense.com

Service Sleuths
servicesleuths.com/
www.mymysteryshop.com/shoppers/LoginShopper.php

Service Solutions, Inc.
www.ssishops.com/ShopperApp.htm
https://servicesolutions.clientsmart.com/

ServiceTRAC (only looking for 50+)
www.servicetrac.com

Service With Style
www.ServiceWithStyle.com
observer.servicewithstyle.com/

SG Marketing Group
www.sglevelabove.com/shoppers/LoginShopper.php
https://www.sassieshop.com/2sgmarketing/index.norm.php

The Shadow Agency
www.theshadowagency.com/

Shop N Check
www.shopnchekshopper.com

Shoppers Confidential
www.shoppersconfidential.com/

Shoppers Critique
https://www.shopperscritique.com

Shop4results
www.shop4results.com

Shoppers, Inc.
www.shopperjobs.com

Shopper's View
www.shoppersview.com

Shopping By Mystery
www.shoppingbymystery.com

ShopServation
shopservation.com/shoppers.html

Sights On Service/Secret Shopper
https://www.secretshopper.com

Signature Worldwide
www.signatureworldwide.com/

Sinclair Service Assessments
www.ssanet.com

Sneak Peakms
spbon.com

The Soloman Group
www.thesolomongroup.com

Speedmark Information Services
www.speedmarkvision.com/shoppers/LoginShopper.php

Spies in Disguise
www.spiesindisguise.com

Strategic Reflections
www.strategicreflections.com

Sullivan/Luallin
www.sullivan-luallin.com

Superior Product Pickup Service

www.productpickup.com
Email: recruiting@productpickup.com

Support Financial Services
www.serviceexperiences.com

-T-
Target Mystery Shoppers (Canada)
members.tripod.com/~Mystery_Shoppers/

Tell Us About Us
www.tellusaboutus.com
www.sassieshop.com/2tuau/index.norm.php
Test Track Research
www.testtrackresearch.com

TNS Intersearch
www.tns-global.com/
www.sassieshop.com/2tns/shoppers/LoginShopper.php

TNS Media Intelligence
www.rapidchek.com

TNS Mystery Shopping
tns.clientsmart.com

Trend Source
www.trendsource.com/
www.msishopper.net

Total Research Solutions
www.trsempower.com

-U-
Undercover Consultants
www.undercoverconsultant.com/
US Mystery Shoppers
usmysteryshoppers.com/

-V-
Video Eyes
www.videoeyes.net/

-W-

Web Mystery Shoppers
www.webmysteryshoppers.com

We Need (Mystery Shoppers)
www.weneed.com/

West Coast Mystery Shopping
www.westcoastmysteryshopping.com

The Woods Group
www.woodsgroupinc.com

-Z-

Zellman Group
www.zellmangroup.com/index2.html
www.sassieshop.com/2zellmangroup/shoppers/LoginShopper.norm.php

Printed in Great Britain
by Amazon